By the same author
Asylum Bound

Although Stuart Townsend has a background in psychiatry, since retiring he has spent as much time as he is allowed touring the Great War battlefields, especially Verdun.

He lives in Nottinghamshire, England with his long suffering wife, but tours regularly with his eldest son or his best friend, both of whom are better navigators!

His other interests are rugby, bridge, beer, pub quizzes and golf.

This is his second book.

Pocket Guide

to the

Battlefields

of

Verdun

Stuart Townsend

CONTENTS

Foreword

When I first visited Verdun I had to rely on World War One "historians" and "anoraks" to point the way to the best sites. Often I found the general area but failed to find the specific

site. As time went on I discovered the best sites, but only with a great deal of time spent in the pub (oh, what a sufferance), annoying the boffins by demanding exact locations. Verdun is so very different from The Somme or Ypres which have routes, road maps and recommendations gleaned over decades. It took friends and relatives to suggest this gap in the bibliography of the Great War could and should be filled.

My first book, Asylum Bound, looked at the oddities and disturbances of the English mental hospitals of the 1970s. Verdun of the Great War seems to connect in my mind – a mix of the brave and the thoughtful, with the absurd and the violent. Both would shape people forever, mostly negatively, though allegiances and friendships would be formed which would stay strong.

This book was both a labour of love and a novel excuse to escape to the Lorraine region to wander these mesmerising battlefields on the Meuse. And my hope? To enthuse you with my conviction that the sites of Verdun, once a nightmare in the Great War, are now a dream - they are simply unparalleled elsewhere.

Once visited they will be cemented in your memory for ever.

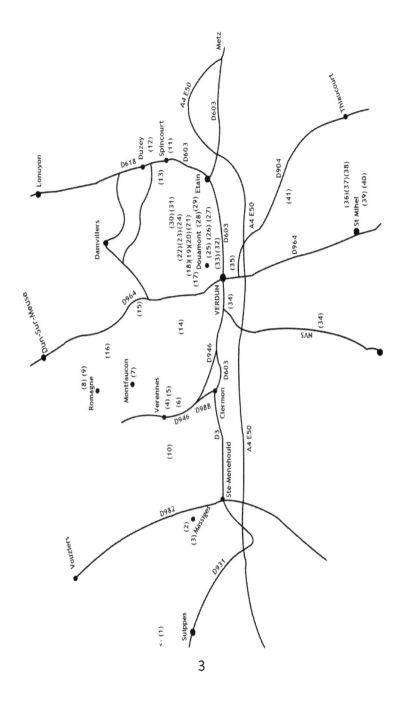

3

Introduction

So, you have visited The Somme and the Flanders areas of France. Now you are visiting Verdun and its surroundings. You have chosen well!

For many years I visited The Somme and the Ypres Salient, getting to know the battlefields, the museums and the memorials. Yet, as I introduced others to these fascinating Great War sites, I was aware that there was another iconic area on the Western Front which I had left unseen and unexplored –

Verdun.

Rather reluctantly I agreed to just one trip to the area, an area which was considerably further afield than Albert and Ypres, and which possibly had less to offer to a British citizen. Surely one trip would be enough. My enthusiasm was underwhelming. I was aware that, unlike the huge memorials of Thiepval,

The Menin Gate and Vimy Ridge, there was little of this magnitude in the Verdun area. So perhaps it might be a tad boring....

How wrong could I be?

From my many trips to the Great War battlefields of Flanders my favourite site is the Sanctuary Wood Museum outside Ypres, with its relatively unaltered trench system. It is

here that wellington boots are needed and, in a rainy autumn, it's a muddy visit with trenches and tunnels which are not overly tidied up and rehashed for the school trips. It's the most down and dirty area in the Ypres Salient – if you half close your eyes you can just about imagine what it might have been like. It's the place to get my torch out.

As I made my first trip to Verdun I hoped that the lack of big memorials might be balanced by a few of these types of grubby, original trenches. It was.

The trench systems around Verdun will 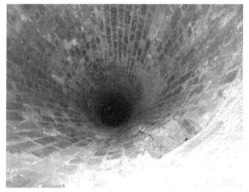 simply stagger you. It is as if you are the first person to have found them, untouched after a century, with all the flotsam and jetsam scattered for your eyes only. Here are trench and tunnel systems still being discovered - still scattered with Great War detritus. This is a place for the wellington boots to be pulled on in the morning and only taken off before the trip to the pub in the evening. This is the place where a torch is mandatory – the only way of finding your route safely in and out.

A trip to Verdun is seeing the Great War in the raw. Indeed, you may need a maxillofacial surgeon as it is, quite simply, jaw dropping.

But let me issue a warning: the sites around Verdun are, to say the least, often under-prepared. Indeed some are without any instructions or signs, certainly lacking any rudiments of health and safety. Let me go further and say that there are some sites around Verdun, not listed here, which are prohibited completely to the public – though the enthusiasts still go. In many areas there are tunnel entrances in the ground unprotected by grills, structures with dangerous rotting roofs, ordinance left untended. I would always say that most outdoor sites around Verdun shouldn't be visited alone.

After the battle subsided around Verdun assessments were made about what could have been done better. During the height of the battle communications became almost impossible between the forts, ouvrages,

headquarters and trenches. Telephone wires

were quickly severed by shelling, leading to uncoordinated action. Forts which were surrounded by enemy troops had no option but to surrender – there was no escape. The result of this was the commencement of the Travaux 17, the building of deep tunnels to link the forts with an escape route and a communications system for the future. These tunnels started everywhere – horses and stable doors come to mind - but the French lost interest in the project at the end of the war and many of these tunnels, incomplete and unsafe, still survive. Hence please watch where you tread. This is potentially a very dangerous place.

There may be a tendency to see these Verdun sites as areas to find and retrieve iron harvest, i.e. bits of the war left from a hundred years ago. However, this isn't the Somme or Ypres and the police will vigourously prosecute. It is considered that the whole battlefield around Verdun is one vast mass grave and if you are caught engaging in metal detecting or taking iron harvest, or are found with a metal detector or 'souvenirs' in your possession, you face a huge fine of thousands of euros, your car can be confiscated and you may even end up as a "guest of the President"! Be warned.

In this book there is a short history of the Great War as it affected Verdun. This will give you a shape for what you see as well as introducing you to some of the key figures you will come across. Following this are routes to take; north, south, east and west.

The fanatic will say that each takes about a week. However, I've set this out so that you can choose what to do, and in what depth. If you only have a couple of days in total then at least you'll get a good flavour of the area, with a variety of activities and places to visit.

You will be back.

What's not in this book

The last time I was in Verdun town I met a very intense anorak chappy in the pub, L'Estaminet, who was on his thirty fifth trip to the area. Not only did he know ALL the sites but I think he probably knew the names of each soldier serving in that area! In Verdun there are going to be specialists. This isn't a specialist book and it doesn't pretend to be. Neither is it a history book, nor is it a definitive guide to everything. It's a guide for those who are still quite new to the area, or for those who have only seen some of the sites. It gives a brief history of the battle, to put it in context, and more than forty of the best sites, as well as coordinates for all the forts and ouvrages.

Unlike the Somme or Flanders areas, the Verdun region is not well signed. Given my own experience of getting lost on a very regular basis, I've tried to ensure the places are findable. On my first trip to Verdun I was given little choice of where to go and what to see. The recommended books were either very heavy tomes, or in French, or Verdun was only included as a brief after-thought to books about Flanders and The Somme. Everything else was a mere pamphlet. What I wanted was a simple guide – but there were none. What I wanted was available for The Somme or Flanders, but not for Verdun - hence this book.

I've tried to give some sense of what is really worth seeing and what is not. I admit to a degree of subjectivity in this – but I've talked with many others and this is more of a consensus than a single view. This book is for those who wish to see this area, but don't necessarily want to undertake a Verdun Ph.D.

Where an entrance fee is required I have informed you. Compared to Flanders and the Somme, the entrance fees are minimal. Costings only escalate when you choose to have a paid person to guide you - very pricey!

What to take

A raincoat (it is often rainy there), wellington boots (many of the sites are sodden and the tunnels and forts are often filled with water), mosquito repellent (it can be rather an itchy place in season), two good torches (most tunnels and forts have no lighting, so one of those million candle power jobs is best, but always carry a pen torch also), a compass (to find your way back) and a packed lunch - refreshment places are few and far between. Some of my friends take ropes with them in case they slip into a hole and can't get out. I have to say that I, rather daringly, go ropeless!

I am assuming that you have a car, so I have given coordinates for the best sites, many of which do not have an address. Therefore a SatNav with GPS coordinates – really worth buying if you've not got one - will make it so much easier to get to the best places.

How to get there

Head south from Calais to Reims on the A26 and this will lead you to the A4 around and south of Reims to Verdun. This is the quickest direct route and it takes about three and a half hours. The tolls cost about €30 in total.

If you come off at Reims be aware that Reims can get slightly snarled up. However, by going from Reims to Suippes you can pick up much of the western sector.

Calais to Verdun, via the motorway, is about 250 miles. There are lots of "Aires" (motorway stops) along the way to stop and have a coffee.

Verdun and where to stay

The Verdun region is amazingly underpopulated. Apart from the town of Verdun there are no other towns of any size. Drive from Verdun northwards and it will seem as if you are on little more than single carriage way roads. But then you'll usually be the only vehicle on the road anyway.

Luckily Verdun is a lovely town and has many places to stay, most of which, unlike the hotels in Ypres or Albert, are relatively cheap. The hotels in the centre, typically, are slightly more expensive and parking is more difficult. The ones further away are cheaper but less convenient for the pub. The centre of Verdun is the size of a small English market town, so don't think that there's bound to be lots of suburbs with bars and restaurants. There aren't. Verdun doesn't have a great choice in hotels, but all the ones I've stayed in are very friendly, adequate and relatively cheap – though sometimes about as spacious as the international space station. You won't find you need them for anything other than a shower and a bed to lay your weary head.

Verdun itself has a beautiful frontage of bars

and cafes along the Quay de Londres (so called because the English paid towards its development after the war, leaving a red telephone box as a farewell gift!). Follow the quay towards the Porte Chaussee (Old Gate House) and, on the left, you will find Bar L'Estaminet (open Tues – Sat) with real ale and probably a clan of British battlefield gurus. This is a great place to get the latest news of what's worth seeing. The other bar which always seems open is the Bar Le Point Central on the corner of the Rue de la Chaussee and Rue Mazel. Be aware that many bars and restaurants close on Sundays and Mondays – quite why is beyond me!

The Office de Tourism is on the other side of the river from the old gatehouse. Do drop in on them – they are very knowledgeable, friendly and speak great English - if only to get a free map.

The Story of Verdun in
The Great War

At the start of the First World War Verdun was ten miles from the German border. The

French had lost territory to the Germans after their defeat in the Franco-Prussian War which ended in 1871, with Verdun the last town to surrender to the occupying German forces.

After that war, with the threat of further attack, the French decided to fortify the surrounds of Verdun with a series of about 45 forts and ouvrages (smaller forts) circling the town in two concentric defensive rings. The largest of these, Fort Douaumont to the east, was thought by both the Allied and Axis Powers to be impregnable. This became a honeypot the Germans wanted.

The Great War was about 18 months old. The Western Front, the long line of trenches from the channel to Switzerland, had become static. Both sides were asking the big question - how to deliver the knock-out blow?

General Eric Von Falkenhayn, the Chief of the German General Staff, reviewed the situation in 1915 and decided that Britain was the main threat to Germany. In order to defeat Britain, he thought, France had first to be knocked out of the war. Once this was done, he concluded, Britain would be forced to sue for peace.

To accomplish this defeat of France he decided that the area around Verdun, a town with an almost sacred status, a town the French revered for its stolid defence against Germany in the Franco-Prussian War, should be attacked. Verdun was already in a salient, with German troops to its south, north, west and north-east. The French were almost surrounded there already, and they would have been best to abandon it and straighten the trench line, but Falkenhayn knew they'd never voluntarily retreat from their Verdun.

So Verdun was to be the trap to pull the French Army into the area. Falkenhayn knew that this almost mythical status of Verdun - it was the very symbol of resistance in France - would require the French army to pour into its defence and so, by the attrition of his huge artillery pieces, he could "bleed France white". He estimated that he could slaughter the French at a rate of five French deaths for every two Germans. All he had to do was to hold the high ground and allow the French to attack. The big guns on the hills surrounding Verdun would do their terrible work.

The German Fifth Army, which was chosen to make the offensive, was commanded by Kaiser Wilhelm's son, the Crown Prince Wilhelm, and the Kaiser watched his rather spoilt son with enthusiasm. The Crown Prince (or the *Clown Prince* as the English newspapers called him), rather

than following the plans of his superior officer, Falkenhayn, decided unilaterally that he wanted to capture the town of Verdun itself - definitely not a part of the grand plan – seeking the glory of its capture rather than the hard slog of attrition which was planned.

The failure of the Germans to break through the existing more northern part of the Western Front meant that this new front would be the

German focus for 1916. Once the French soldiers were in place, massed to defend the area, they could be destroyed by the heavy guns brought up for the destruction of the French army by Germany. So General Falkenhayn decided that Verdun was to be the charnel house for the French army.

For the French, however, the pressure in 1915 had been on the more northern parts of the Western Front, especially around the Champagne area. Therefore during the summer of 1915 armaments, both guns and munitions, had been taken away from the forts of Verdun and moved to those pressure points further north. The Germans, as well as the French General Staff, were unaware how pitifully weak the Verdun region had become.

From the experience of Ypres and the Champagne area the French knew that even highly fortified structures couldn't withstand the heavy shelling from Germany's new 16.5 inch guns, and so had reduced the forts and ouvrages to mere connecting points for trenches. Despite reinforced concrete walls it had been found that the simple earth was more resistant to heavy shells, absorbing the impact better. Trenches also provided smaller, less obvious targets. However, due to the pressures on the more northern trenches on the Western Front, the systems of trenches around Verdun had also failed to be upgraded and strengthened. The Germans did not know that they were about to push at an open door.

In January and early February 1916 the Germans had secretly been massing troops

and heavy guns around Verdun, with new

railway lines and railway platforms built to take men and munitions quickly to the new front. Guns from all over Germany were brought together – 1,200 of them. German deserters who slipped across the lines into the French sector told of the massive build-up of men and munitions. They warned of something truly terrible to come.

They were not wrong.

In January 1916 the General Headquarters (GHQ) of the French army started to worry about Verdun and its lack of preparedness. General Joffre, Commander in Chief of the French Army, received a letter from GHQ stating that it had come to their attention that the line of trenches round Verdun had not been completed, warning that General

GENERAL JOFFRE

Joffre himself was responsible if anything were to be found wanting. Joffre replied that they had nothing to fear, whilst quickly sending a regiment of engineers to strengthen the trench systems on the eastern bank of the Meuse.

Luckily for the French, the planned date of the attack, February 11th, was postponed due to poor weather conditions. This ten day delay allowed for the trenches to be upgraded and for reinforcements to come to the defence of Verdun.

Two new divisions were moved up, veterans of the fighting further north. They were nicknamed "Poilus", the Hairy Ones, for their whiskery appearance – a term equivalent to the British "Tommy". They knew their chance of survival was slim as they were now receiving more information about the huge build-up of arms and munitions on the German side, ready for the onslaught.

On 21st February 1916 the Germans launched their initial bombardment around Verdun, with over two million shells, in six hours. A further three million were fired over the next two weeks.

The descriptions of this attack make difficult reading, with graphic reports describing the impact of shells on the human body.

"The crude iron of the shells shattered into huge ragged chunks which sometimes two men would be unable to lift. Men were squashed, cut in two, or divided from top to bottom, blown into showers, bellies turned inside out and scattered anyhow. Skulls were forced bodily into the chest, as if hit by a blow with a club".

 As the German guns stopped, so the German ground forces attacked, overwhelming the front trenches of the French. For this assault the Germans were experimenting with a new weapon, the flamethrower - burning oil propelled by compressed nitrogen - now used to terrify and burn through the defences. French soldiers were the first to become flaming torches in this appalling war. However, although the flame-throwers were a psychological as well as physical weapon, as time went on the French started to learn about their weaknesses, focusing their gun sights on the carrier – finding that a well-aimed bullet would take out not just the soldier, but often his many comrades as the thrower fell and twisted, unleashing the deadly spray randomly.

The Germans took over 10,000 prisoners in this first assault. They were soon through the frontline trenches and into open country. They had started to capture the high ground of the hills around Verdun. But the forts and ouvrages still stood. More French soldiers were rushed to the front.

On 27th February, just six days after the start of the campaign, ten combat engineers from the Brandenburg regiment, led by a Sergeant Kunze, managed to approach the honeypot of Fort Douaumont. The weather was poor and the few French soldiers in the fort who were on lookout thought that the approaching Germans were French colonial

Pioneer Sergeant Kunze

troops returning from patrol, so failed to see a threat. Entering the moat Kunze found an open access door and encouraged his men to follow. His men refused, thinking that it looked like a trap – it was far too easy – so Kunze went in alone. Finding the French artillery team in the basement, having a quiet meal, he locked them up without firing a shot. Now other German soldiers joined him and quickly they secured the surrender of the entire fort.

The fort, defended by fifty six elderly soldiers and no officers, had fallen. (Interestingly a wounded Charles de Gaulle was captured around the

same time near here, to spend the next 32 months as a POW). The popular view had been that Fort Douaumont was the most impregnable fortress in the world. It wasn't. The capture of the fort was a propaganda triumph for the Germans who promptly announced a public holiday.

The French public wasn't told of its fall – just that fighting around the fort was intense. For some days the French government continued to deny its fall, despite evidence seeping through to Paris. But at last they had to admit the catastrophe. The disgrace of its fall was a national disaster for the French High Command. It has been estimated that it took 100,000 French lives to win back their treasured Fort Douaumont.

With this national catastrophe the French High Command, under General Joffre, decided that one man had to organise the defence of Verdun. General Philippe Petain was now appointed to take immediate charge of its defence. The first problem was that no one could find him. It took considerable pressure on his trusted aide in order even to find Petain as he was in bed with his mistress in Paris for his weekly pleasures, and only the aide knew which hotel. He was none too pleased at being disturbed! Once he reached the area of Verdun he fell ill with pneumonia and those around him didn't think he'd survive. However he pulled through to begin the task of holding out against the Germans.

On the whole he was a popular choice, with soldiers thinking that perhaps he cared more for his common soldiers than other generals. One of the first actions he took was to organize that French soldiers would be rotated at the front, having no more than eight days there before a rest.

Yet you will find that Petain, despite his brilliant defense of Verdun, is a figure who is rarely referred to in the history of the battle, or at the sites you visit - quietly and humanely airbrushed from the story, a popular soldier who became an national embarrassment

He is the forgotten commander. Petain was the "hero" of the French after the Great War but later became the head of the French government of Vichy France after their surrender in 1940, making shady deals with Hitler, including rounding up Jews for transportation. So, after his downfall at the end of the Second World War, he was condemned to death by a French court for treason, though his  sentence was later commuted to exile. He is buried on an island off the coast of Brittany, never to return to his mainland France. One senses he's an ongoing source of French embarrassment in Verdun, both hero and traitor - a difficult combination.

The Germans, now jubilant about their capture of the mighty Fort Douaumont quickly found that it was a pyrrhic victory.

Fort Douaumont brought nothing but problems for the Germans.

 The first problem was that the fort had been heavily reinforced on the eastward side, i.e. the side the Germans would attack, but had not been as strongly reinforced on the western (French) side. Of course, this softer western side was where the French started to fire their own shells on the Germans – now settling into their new barracks. The western side soon began to be the target for heavy French artillery pieces.

The second problem was that the Germans, unlike the French, decided to pack the fort with its own soldiers and munitions. On 8 May 1916 the Germans, intending to brew up some coffee for the men, and without heating fuel, had decided to use the fuel from a flamethrower as cooking fuel - not a good idea. The high octane fuel quickly caused a fire which led to grenades exploding, leading to the detonation of large amounts of heavier munitions. A firestorm ensued. Many German soldiers, though badly burned, fled from the conflagration. The German soldiers protecting the fort above the firestorm, seeing men in tattered unidentifiable clothing, faces blackened by fire damage, mistook them for

French African soldiers, who they dreaded. They opened up with machine guns slaughtering most of their own men who were escaping. When the chaos had subsided it was found that about 680 German soldiers had been killed. Most of the charred corpses were buried behind a wall in the fort and a memorial placed in front of the bricked up tunnel – still there today.

Yet despite these setbacks, the Germans were slowly throttling the town of Verdun with a creeping success in taking more of the

surrounding hills.

As a result of this almost complete  encirclement of Verdun, the only way into or out of the town for the French was a road and railway from the south, from Bar-Le-Duc, fifty miles away. A narrow-gauge railway and a single track road, twenty feet wide, had now become the main connection between the town and the remainder of France. Trucks, brought in from all over France, running on steel rims due to a shortage of rubber, threaded their way toward Verdun in a long slow caterpillar. The road became known as La Voie Sacree - The Sacred Way (still called this on the road signs). You will probably come in this way.

The Meuse River, running north to south through the Verdun region, became a northern objective for the Germans. They wanted to cross the river just north of Verdun and attack from the northwest, encircling Verdun itself.

To achieve this they had to capture the ominously named hill, Le Mort Homme – The Dead  Man. The area around Le Mort Homme and Côte 304 (Hill 304) became another killing ground, with gas used extensively as well as colossal mines set off from huge tunnel systems. The area was fought over, lost, recaptured and lost again. Côte 304 was said to have lost about 10 meters in height as a result of the bombardments.

Reports of how bad it was in this area can be seen in the letters from soldiers to their families. They reported that the dead were no longer buried – there was little point as the shells merely disinterred them – and of how the corpses were just rolled into another shell

hole. Soldiers using the shell holes for battles were rarely alone, with cadavers and body parts scattered around them. Wounded men were drowned in their shell-holes. As the rain came, they watched as the waters rose – unable to escape a slow and lingering death.

From quite early on in the battle the dressing stations at the front were also unable to cope. Dying men were left outside to die in the cold and wet as there was insufficient space inside.

It is estimated that most wounded men would have to wait five days before treatment could start. Anaesthesia, as well as food, was scarce by this time, so many operations – and the common ones were amputations – had to be done without pain relief. Squads of soldiers were assigned just to keep the rats from gnawing the faces off the wounded men lying outside dressing stations. This was a very unpleasant battle.

The front was extending, becoming a closing salient, with shells hitting the French from three sides.

By the end of March 1916, the Germans and the French had each lost around forty thousand men. Fort Vaux, just a few miles from the huge Fort Douaumont, fell in June after a terrible battle which moved from outside the fort to inside – initially with the Germans on one floor and the French in another – then fighting in the same unlit corridors and tunnels, before its surrender.

In May General Petain was replaced by his second in command, General Nivelle, along

with Nivelle's deputy, General Mangin. Nivelle was less popular among the soldiers than Petain, who felt that he was more profligate and less caring than his predecessor. Nivelle's case wasn't helped by his deputy. Mangin was nicknamed "the Butcher" by the French soldiers, as well as being forever hated by the Germans – though not just because he was a violent attack dog. After the war, during the occupation of the Rhineland by the French, Mangin had insisted that German mayors provide German women as prostitutes for his Senegalese troops, ("German women are none too good for my Senegalese"). Mangin didn't exactly make himself or Nivelle popular and when he died, aged just 58, it was rumoured he'd been murdered by poison.

It was Nivelle's job to go on the attack and drive the Germans back to their start position. He and Mangin were later accused of wasting French lives - a huge escalation of battlefield deaths for no result, his legacy (definitely not helped by Mangin's strapline of "whatever you do you lose a lot of men"). It is also interesting that Hitler, following his notorious visit to Paris  after its fall in 1940 ordered two Parisian memorials to be completely destroyed. One was of General Mangin, for his statement about the sexual morals of German women, and the other, oddly, that of our own Nurse Edith Cavell.

41

The Germans moved on to the last of their original objectives, the village of Fleury and Fort Souville in June, with Nivelle issuing his now famous order "Ils ne passeront pas" (they shall not pass!). The casualty rate soared. Nivelle (along with his side-kick Mangin) was later accused of being the primary reason for why so many troops mutinied in 1917. No surprise there then!

However, by July, the Somme offensive had been launched in order to take the pressure off Verdun, putting increased pressure on the

Germans to hold the line a hundred miles further up the Western Front. German munitions and guns were now diverted to this

Somme offensive area. The Germans had no more reinforcements to maintain the offensive around Verdun. The German line had advanced to within two miles of Verdun itself. Yet even now the slaughter didn't stop, with Fleury, in July, changing hands sixteen times.

But by August and September the German attack had faltered – it had now become a defence. Slowly the tide turned. Germany was running out of supplies. Their focus now was elsewhere – the Somme. The French slowly and painfully retook both Fort Vaux and then Fort Douaumont. The Verdun escapade had come to an end with both sides exhausted.

The Battle of Verdun is considered to have ended in December. Gradually, over the next two years, all areas lost were recaptured by the French, in the later stages with the help of the USA who had, by then, entered the war.

The Battle of Verdun lasted ten months and permanently scarred the people of France by its appalling slaughter. The total casualty figures for the battle have been put at 976,000, though if one puts the total casualties for Verdun during the whole of the Great War it comes to around 1,250,000. The casualties were relatively evenly spread between the French and Germans – it was never even close to the projected 5-2 of Falkenhayn's prediction.

Many historians argue that the speedy surrender of the French in World War Two was due to their memories of the catastrophe

happening here - not being able to face another Verdun. Alistair Horne suggests in his book that the conditions and terror of Verdun were the worst in the annals of human combat – even worse than Stalingrad.

Horne has also assessed that the total area captured by the Germans in the Battle of Verdun was less than the acreage of the London Parks - such a small area for such a massive death toll.

And what of the region around Verdun? It was mostly left alone. The town was rebuilt but much of the rest was slowly left to rot. Ignoring it might let the people forget. Whole villages had disappeared – now called the Destroyed Villages – never to be rebuilt.

The region today is eerie and pockmarked. There are large areas where it is rare to hear wildlife, to see a bird fly, or to see small animals and insects. The fauna seem to have packed their bags and departed. There is a deathly stillness and quiet - a tranquility which brings no comfort. Much of what remains is as it was at the end of the war, but more overgrown. As you wander the trenches and tunnels I'm sure you will feel the battlefields as much as see them.

The Sites

I have divided the sites around Verdun into north, south, east and west. Each of these is a car journey to an area where there are options of what you'd like to visit. The map gives a rough idea of where each site is, so that you can tailor your own trip.

There are official guides who will take you to tunnel and trench systems, but they aren't cheap (300+ Euros per day). This book will get you to all the best ones. But be aware there are some tunnels which only official guides are allowed to enter with tourists – so you may pay extra for these.

After the lists of sites I have included the names and coordinates of all forts and ouvrages around Verdun – a long list but worth stopping to see the untouched hulks.

The battlefield areas can be divided into six types of places to visit:

1. <u>Memorials (MEM)</u> – after the war many memorials were built and I have tried to highlight some of the best.

2. <u>Trenches, Tunnels and Craters (TTC)</u> - these are the most original and untouched remains you will ever see on the whole of the Western Front. Take a torch.

3. <u>Cemeteries (CEM)</u> – French, American and German.

4. <u>Forts and Ouvrages (FAO)</u> The forts and ouvrages were built after the Franco-Prussian War to protect the nearest town, Verdun, from the small border French with Germany. They encircled Verdun in two concentric rings, along

with batteries and linked fortifications. These are all listed fully on page 110ff. Many are on MoD land, but can be viewed. Some were rebuilt and some are now ruins, but they are fascinating. They generally aren't clean, aren't lit and most of them will drip water on you! Some are very, very unsafe. Do ensure you do your own risk assessment before entering.

5. <u>Museums (MUS)</u> Most museums require entrance fees. However all the ones listed here are really worthwhile.

6. <u>Destroyed Villages (DV)</u> After the war ended the destruction to certain areas of the battlefield was so great, so complete, that the French Government decided not to try to rebuild nine villages which were almost untraceable. These nine villages, Beaumont, Bezonvaux,

Cumieres, Douaumont, Haumont, Louvremont, Ornes, Vaux and Fleury became memorials to the destruction of the Great War. They are now signed and marked out, with each presented in a different way. All are really worth a visit – they don't take long to see – and all are fascinating for their before and after photos. Fleury, Bezonvaux and Ornes are my favourites, but if you're driving past do drop in and have a look.

Each site is numbered both on the sites and on the map. The Douaumont enclave is crowded with sites, hence the crowding of numbers and every site has both latitude/longitude and decimal coordinates to help in navigation.

So, choose your sector – north, south, east or west. I would recommend a nice mix of each. Enjoy it!

Verdun Town

Verdun is a small town, easily walkable, with plenty of parking spaces – though don't forget to put your euros in the meter.

The <u>Victory Monument</u> in the Centre of the town depicts Charlemagne resting on his broadsword. Remarkably, there is a museum inside – very small. A lady took an equally small admission fee, for this tiny museum. Bizarre but memorable!

Monument to the Sons of Verdun – sculpture by the river.

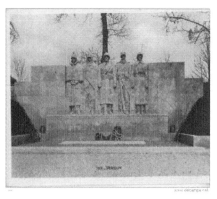

Verdun Cathedral is up the hill above the Victory Monument – worth seeing for the crypt and the very ornate marble edifice over the high altar.

Porte Chaussee, the gate house, on the side of the river Meuse, which dates from the 14th century.

Citadel Souterraine (Children's ride!) Expensive ride on a dodgem trolley around a cave with various filmed recreations (though the acting leaves a lot to be desired). Save yourself and your money!

Faubourg Pave French Cemetery

Coordinates: 49°09'51N,   005°24'17E   –
49.16416, 5.40472

This cemetery, on the N18 road to Etain, the way to the battlefields, includes seven aviators from  GB and Canada. The cemetery also has a number of French field guns – well worth a look as you'll be passing it anyway.

The Western Sector

Fort de la Pompelle (MUS FAO) (1)
Address: 51500 Puisieuix
Coordinates: 49°12'58N, 004°07'36E – 49.21611, 4.12666

This site is perhaps best seen either on the way to Verdun or on the way back, as it is just outside Reims, which you will almost certainly travel through. Travelling from Rheims towards Verdun, leave Reims by the D980 and you will pass this fort. Unlike Fort Douaumont this fort is clean, tidy and so perhaps less interesting! There is a short film and the fort spreads beyond the museum part. The most interesting exhibits I found to be the dress German helmets, which are well worth having a good look at, with some which seem like mortar board helmets and others with the death's head. There is a small entrance fee, not expensive, but don't make this your only fort. Overall this is a tidy and neat fort with good displays. But it isn't earthy Verdun. Allow one hour.

Main de Massiges (TTC) (2)

Address: La Main de Massiges, 51800, Massiges

Coordinates: 49°11'41"N, 004°45'16"E – 49.194722, 4.75444

The Main de Massiges is on the left hand side when travelling from Suippes towards Verdun, on the D66. It's a remarkable place to catch on your way from Reims to Verdun. If you haven't a SatNav there is a signpost to the site in the middle of the village itself. There is a car park, though almost certainly you'll be the only car there, and the site is ahead of you. It is free to enter but you'll need boots and a torch.

This is a site that is being developed by

volunteers and, though it is already very large, there is much still to be found. Remains of fallen soldiers have been found here. I understand that after the war the system was covered in lime by the farmers and abandoned. It is only in the past few years that it has been extensively excavated. There are a couple of signboards, but not much else. The vista tells you all you need to know. If it's raining it's very muddy and the copious barbed wire ripped my umbrella to shreds. Detritus and iron harvest litters the ground – obviously leave it well alone. It's an absolute treat of a site. Allow 1 hour.

Minaucourt French Cemetery (CEM) (3)
Address: Minaucourt-le-Mesnil-lès-Hurlus
Coordinates: 49°10'51"N, 004°43'35"E – 49.180833, 4.726388

Close to Main de Massiges on the D566, here more than 8,000 French soldiers are buried, along with a handful or so of British soldiers.

U.S.A. Pennsylvania Memorial (MEM) (4)

Address:
Varennes-en-
Argonne
Coordinates:
49°13'30"N,
005°01'54"E –
49.22555, 5.0325
The
Pennsylvania

Memorial, a monument for volunteers from 28th Division Pennsylvania in the First World War, was erected in Varennes during the Interwar period. It's a huge memorial, two walls in white stone, and is impressive though difficult to photograph. There's a great view over the valley at the rear of the memorial. If you are going to the Varennes Museum then make sure you see this, which is next door. It's a sleepy little village and worth a wander anyway.

Varennes Museum (d'Argonne) (MUS) (5)

Address: Varennes-en-Argonne

Coordinates: 49°13'30"N, 005°01'54"E - 49.22555, 5.0325

This museum is next door to the Pennsylvania Memorial. It consists of three sections – only one of which is related to the Great War -

specialising in mine warfare. There is a small entrance charge (about 5€) and it seems to be shut most mornings, but we found 2-4 the best time to ensure it was open. There seems to be an optional aspect about the opening times of sites in the area, so never feel anything is definite! Allow about 1 hour.

Butte de Vauquois (MUS TTC) (6)
Address: 55270 Vauquois
Coordinates: 49°12'21"N, 005°04'12"E –
41.20583, 5.06999
This is my favourite place in the Verdun
region. Aim for Varennes, follow the D212
and the signs. Torch most definitely needed.

There are tunnels crisscrossing the site with
many still to be discovered and excavated.
This is, again, an area under construction.
There are some wonderful old photos here as
well as large amounts of mining equipment.
On exiting the museum cross the road and

walk to the right of the shelter on the lower

path. This will take you to the lower end of the site, crossing into the German trenches and tunnel entrances. Be careful as there are exposed tunnels without grills. Follow upwards, through the trench systems, until you reach the height of the hill. Here you will find the series of craters photographed. They are staggeringly deep. Follow these upwards. Then cross to the other side of the hill where the French were defending. Cut past the memorial and down the track. On the left, in the woods, are further tunnels (some of which are very lengthy, deep and need a guide) and a railway system. You will see work continuing on various areas, but they always seem covered in tarpaulins. Here are further trench systems. Search around and you'll find

all sorts of visual treasures. There is a display of blockhouse construction methods at the entrance which is also worth a glimpse. At the time of writing the deeper tunnels are open every first Sunday of the month from 0930-Midday, for a small fee. If you can time your visit for this it's really worth it. And if you only have the time for one trench site, this is the one. Be amazed, but be careful.

Overall a magnificent site. There is a small entrance charge to the museum. Allow about 2 hours.

Butte de Montfaucon (MEM) (DV) (7)

Address: Montfaucon d'Argonne

Coordinates: 49°16'21"N, 005°08'30"E – 49.2725, 5.14166

This huge Doric column, built in the 1930s, is a memorial to the USA servicemen who fought and died in the area in the last month of the Great War in the Meuse-Argonne

Offensive. It has over two hundred steps, with fourteen floors, to the top – it is a very long way up to viewing area - giving a great vista of the surrounding battlefield. The winds up there seemed tornado speed, so cling on! The tower is topped off with a statue representing Liberty. The memorial is situated at the front of the Destroyed Village of Montfaucon, so do go behind the memorial also where you'll find the broken village and various emplacements and shelters. Allow 1 hour.

U.S.A. Cemetery Meuse-Argonne (CEM) (8)

Address: Rue de General Pershing, 55110 Romagne-sous-Montfaucon

Coordinates: 49°20'03"N, 005°05'36"E – 49.33416, 5.09333

The USA never builds anything small. This is no exception. However, the numbers of

graves point to the fact that, though they were late starters in The Great War – a habit they seemed to get into - once in France they died at the same awful rate as the others. In the chaos of so many sites, the tidiness here is something of a novelty. There appeared to be more gardeners than at Chatsworth. This is the largest US Cemetery in Europe, easily dwarfing the one in Normandy. It covers 130 acres with 14,246 headstones. The Visitor Centre is being completely reorganized, so it's a great place to stop, possibly on the way home. Beautifully laid out cemetery. Don't forget your camera.

Romagne 14-18 Museum (MUS) (9)

Address: 2 rue de l'Andon, 55110, Romagne-sous-Montfaucon

Coordinates: 49°19'56"N, 005°04'58"E – 49.33222, 5.08277

This excellent museum covers the fighting involving the different American and German units that fought in the area around Romagne-sous-Montfaucon during the Great War. Most of the huge collection comes from the surrounding area of the village, and you are allowed to handle most of it. It's housed in a huge barn, and there is a café and also a small shop, legally selling battlefield relics, books and militaria. The owner, Jean-Paul de Vries, is passionate about the Great War - his

knowledge of the area is excellent (and he speaks great English as well as being genuinely friendly!) - so he's well worth chatting with. It opens from 1:00pm to 6:00pm (except Wednesday). There is no entrance charge, but voluntary contributions are usually 5€. Allow 1 hour.

Kaiser Tunnel and Trenches and Memorial to French Soldier (MEM) (TTC) (10)

Address: Argonne Forest D38c

Coordinates: 49°11'19"N, 004°59'38"E – 49.188611, 4.99388

The Kaiser's Tunnel and the Memorial to the French Soldier are deep in the woods. The coordinates  will take you to the memorial, reminiscent of the memorial to the Canadian Soldier near Ypres. Firstly look behind the memorial and there are a line of huge craters. Then head in the opposite direction to the signs pointing to the Kaiser Tunnel.

Cutting through the woods, following the markers, you will go through trenches, many with tunnels and "stollen" (German shelters). Once at the Kaiser Tunnel entrance you will be able to take a photo over the padlocked iron gate which bars your entrance. With a good flash system you should be able to make out the line of downward steps on the other side. You will notice a building opposite. This has been deserted for some time and seems abandoned, except that a small museum still is housed there. Have a good look round. A resupply cart filled with artefacts - bullets and shrapnel inside a flimsy cabinet etc. Behind

this, through the back door, a tunnel disappears to…. No idea! Usual warnings apply here, so please be very careful. The tunnel has been open in the past and there is word it will reopen – but no one seems to know when. Along the road from here keep an eye out for the Crown Prince's HQ (named Abri de Kronprinz) which has fortifications and trenches also. But it's a bit of a walk.

The Northern Sector

Spincourt Railway (11)

Address: Spincourt 55230

Coordinates: 49°19′58″N, 005°40′04″E – 49.33277, 5.66777

Worth a quick look, especially if you are visiting the nearby Long Max Cannon (Site du

Canon Allemand) nearby. The coordinates will take you to one side of the railway track next to the level crossing. Walk to the left, and you'll notice the old railway lines. To their left is the longest platform you'll ever see - about a third of a mile long – built by the Germans for supplying their front. Then cross the railway line (the modern one) at the level crossing and look left for a better view. Continue walking up that road and, if you scramble up the embankment, you'll get a still better view. Coming back notice the bunker on the right past the cross roads. Allow ten minutes.

Long Max Cannon (Site du Canon Allemand) (Bois de Warphemont) (TTC) (12)

Address: Duzey

Coordinates: 49°21′31″N, 005°35′49″E – 49.358611, 5.596944

This takes a bit of finding (though there are signs around Duzey occasionally), but it really is worth it, so fire up your SatNav coordinates and head to the forest. Take your torch and wellies. Again this site just keeps getting better. Initially it looks disappointing - a large blue gun which turns out not to be the original, (had someone nicked the old one for scrap, I wondered?) has been left by the side of the road. The colour is odd – why blue?

But, grab your camera and explore behind the gun. Now you're in amazing territory. There are the tunnels (watery, dark and exciting) where the shells were brought in by rail. Then  there's the base for the gun, with huge bolts which held the gun to the central spindle. Then there's the shell - massive.

Good information signs will keep you on the right track. This was the emplacement for the gun which managed to hit Verdun, reducing much of the town to rubble. A place from where hell was unleashed. Don't miss it. Allow 1 hour.

Camp Marguerre (Abandoned Rest & Recreation area) (13)

Address: Spincourt Wood near Loison

Coordinates: 49°18′38″N, 005°36′43″E – 49.31055, 5.61194

If you get to Loison, near Spincourt, with these coordinates, it will direct you from there. It really is worth finding. This is another  oddity which is uniquely Verdunesque. Be amazed, and just a bit frightened! This camp, made from reinforced concrete slabs, was set up as a rest and recreation area for the Germans well behind the lines. Completely abandoned after the war it rotted until the Second World War when the French Resistance used it briefly as a hideout. Without SatNav I'm pretty sure the Germans would have struggled to find it.

After 1945 it returned to rotting away, far from anywhere. It is situated in a damp, dark wood and the buildings are decaying. In its time it must have been a large village, so there is endless fascination here with houses and

shelters, Great War graffiti, roofs collapsing, all hidden in this forbidding forest. The sign boards, which are informative and useful, fill in the gaps. It is much larger than it first looks as it spreads out deep into the forest. It looks as if it's the set for some very scary movie so keep an eye on where everyone else is, and the other eye on what's behind you! Allow 1 hour.

Mort Homme (TTM MEM) (14)

Address: Chattancourt

Coordinates: 49°13'44"N, 005°15'08"E – 49.22888, 5.25222

By continuing south on the D18 proceed to the monument on Hill 304. The monument is at the end of a long straight tree lined road. To the left of the monument is the tomb of Lt Fabre. Once this is found walk to the left from here and the German front line is visible. This was one of the fiercest fighting areas – fought over, lost, recaptured many times. This is an area worth exploring – the trench lines and pocked earth, the craters… Lots of walks from here, especially to Hill 304 (Cote 304) on a sunny day. Allow 1 hour.

Consenvoye German War Cemetery (15)

Address: Consenvoye

Coordinates: 49°16'46"N, 005°17'47"E – 49.27944, 5.29638

This German cemetery, just south of the village on the road to Verdun, is the largest in the Verdun area with  11,146 graves. Most of the dead were buried in ossuary type mass burial mounds, set at the high point of the cemetery. Also keep an eye out for Jewish graves, with the Star of David - so many died fighting for a nation which had a plan for them in the next war. Certainly worth stopping to see the typical minimalist, rather brutalist, design of so many of these German cemeteries. Allow 10 minutes

----

Brieulles French Cemetery (CEM) (16)

Address: Brieulles

Coordinates: 49°20'05"N, 005°10'23"E – 49.334722, 5.173055

Although quite a small French cemetery, this one, on a slope, is interesting in that there appears to be one solitary British CWGC grave on the lower right to a soldier of the Post Office Rifles. I often wonder what he was doing here, so far from home, and why he is alone. I have, as yet, been unable to find out. Very poignant. Stop by and pay your respects.

The Eastern Sector

<u>Verdun Memorial and Museum (Fleury) (MEM MUS) (17)</u>
Address: Fleury
Coordinates: 49°11'42"N, 005°26'00"E – 49.19499, 5.43333

The major museum of the area and if you're only going to do one museum this is the one. It's been closed for a year for refurbishment, reopening in 1916 for the centenary. The wait has been worthwhile. A really magnificent display. Make sure you spend time watching the computerised terrain map showing how the front lines changed. There are many screens and films, with well-preserved exhibits also. Somehow they've managed to modernise without trivializing. Entrance Charge but very well worth it! Allow 2 hours.

Fleury (DV) (18)
Address: Fleury
Coordinates: 49°11'54"N, 005°25'45"E – 49.19833, 5.42916
This is perhaps the most famous of the Destroyed Villages, near the Verdun Memorial (Fleury) Museum.
Like most of these Destroyed Villages there is an attempt to show where

houses and buildings were situated before they were blown to smithereens. Well worth a look and a wander, with good information boards. The photos I like to examine are the before and after ones, with the shelling erasing a piece of history, but creating another. Photos taken in 1914 show a pretty village, with rows of farm cottages, on a little street. By 1916 Fleury was a wreck with just a few indicators of where houses had been. By 1918 there was nothing left - just mud and craters. It is the rubbing out of history – a metaphor for the Great War. Allow half an hour for the visit.

Fort Douaumont (FAO) (19)
Address: 55100 Douaumont
Coordinates: 49°13'01"N, 005°26'19"E – 49.21694, 5.43861
The largest and most famous of the forts and the central pivot of the defences around Verdun, this is a huge fort, with many floors and endless corridors, all dripping with water. The natural well, with a ladder descending, was so deep I was unable to see the bottom (and I understand that the safety grill is comparatively new!). The gun

emplacement, with its winding system, is an engineering joy. The sense of its vastness only came to me when I'd started in another floor, with more side tunnels, realising I had no idea

where I was in relation to the entrance.

The site has excellent electronic gear, iPods and headphones, for you to wear which will talk you through the fort. You will be offered either the headphones (translated into English) or a pamphlet. I advise wearing the headphones which really give a great commentary - & I'm not usually a fan of high tech - as well as short films from the time. If you are only

going to visit one fort, this is the one. I

discovered that finding my way out, at the end of the tour, was difficult – somebody must have eaten the breadcrumbs! There is an entrance charge, but I recommend the joint ticket for both Fort Douaumont and Fort Vaux - well worth it - with the same technology in each. Allow 1.5 hours.

Douaumont Ossuary (MEM, CEM, MUS) (20)
Address: 55100 Douaumont
Coordinates: 49°12'32"N, 005°25'25"E – 49.20888, 5.42361
The skeletal remains of about 130,000

unidentified soldiers are kept here – both

German and French. The bones are seen through lower windows. The ossuary is still added too as bones are discovered.

Also here is the largest French cemetery of the Great War, with over 16,000 graves. On the inside of the building, bathed in an orange glow are plaques for individual soldiers and an eternal flame. There is a small museum in the tower, the opportunity to climb the main tower (very high!) and see a brilliant short film. There is an entrance charge, but well worth it. Allow 1.5 hours.

The area around Douaumont is scattered with relics and remains, trench systems and craters. I haven't listed them all separately as the best way to see them is to wander in this relatively small area. Much of it is signposted – a rarity in the Verdun battlefields – and the shop in the Ossuary will give you directions as well. It's probably best to do a circuit on foot around the Ossuary and the cemetery and you will cover some wonderful sites.

Ouvrage de Froideterre (FAO) (21) (Coordinates 49°11'51"N, 005°24'13"E – 49.20000, 5.47027) is on the D913.

This ouvrage, which is absolutely huge, consisting of three sections in a crescent shape, changed hands a number of times. As usual the top is covered with earth and grass, so at times it is hard to see how large it really is. The area around is littered with deep shell holes. On the left and right wings of the fort are entrance ways into it – not speaking French I was unsure if this is strictly allowed – and it is

dark, wet, flooded in places, dripping and simply amazing.

The gun systems are still in place along with the cantilevered structures. Also here are the barracks and bunk beds. You must have a torch and entry is at your risk! Around the area shell craters bear witness to the terrible fighting that went on here. Mind blowing. Allow an hour.

Haumont Destroyed Village (DV) (22)

Address: Haumont

Coordinates: 49°16'20"N, 005°21'03"E – 49.272169, 5.350845

This Destroyed Village – different again from any others – has life size photos of figures from the village.

83

They seem like ghostly reminders of the life which once was led here. There are also blockhouses and ruins, a chapel and the usual shell holes. Unlike other Destroyed Villages, I've never seen any other people visiting here, which is a pity as it's lovely and tranquil.

Abri Caverne (23) (The Four Chimneys)

Coordinates 49°11'59"N, 005°24'40"E – 49.19972, 5.41111 (by car) Take a torch as this is a large underground shelter with four huge chimneys protruding from the earth used initially for reserve troops, but then given over to first aid facilities as the battle grew closer. It was attacked by the Germans with grenades thrown down the chimneys. The chaos inside grew worse as flame-throwers were used to kill the wounded sheltering inside, before the French soldiers pushed the Germans back. The Germans finally unleased a massive gas

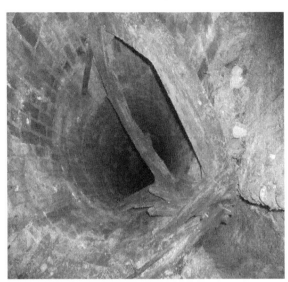

attack, with the gas settling in the shelter killing everyone there, as they had no gas protection. It is the stuff of nightmares. The shelter is open for explorers, but again a torch is a must as it is unlit. Great photos can be taken both down the chimneys and inside the shelter. The signboards give very good information about the area and the shelter. Allow 1 hour for exploring.

Ornes Destroyed Village (DV) (24)

Address: Ornes

Coordinates: 49°15'08"N, 005°28'03"E – 49.252222, 5.467500

This is the only Destroyed Village to be partially rebuilt, with some pillars and parts of major buildings put back to give an impression of what it was like. Good places for photos of the quiet scene.

Fort Thiaumont (FAO TTC) (25)

Coordinates: 49'12.24"N, 5,25.11"E – 49.206666, 5.41972 To the right of the Douaumont Ossuary walking - again this battered ouvrage changed hands fourteen times. It was also here that Green Cross gas shells were first used against the French – a gas which the French gas masks were unable to filter out (and which killed snails, flies and other insects).

Colonel Driant Bunker and Memorial (MEM) (TTC) (26)

Address: Bois de Caures

Coordinates: 49°16'16"N, 005°24'20"E – 49.271111, 5.405555

Head for Bras and turn right at the roundabout, pointed to Bois de Caures. Colonel Driant is one of the few famous heroes of the battle of Verdun. Before the war he was a soldier, writer and politician. However, prior to the war he fell from favour in the higher establishment of France for two reasons. Firstly he was very vocal in stating that the Verdun area was severely weakened following the removal of guns to other areas – something which General Joffre denied. Secondly he married the daughter of a strident nationalist, which became a bar on his promotion to higher rank.

Here in the Bois de Caures he led two infantry battalions (the Chausseurs or Hunters) in the defence of this area on the first day of the battle of Verdun. Despite initially holding the German wave of attack, the Chausseurs had to fall back. Colonel Driant was killed by sniper fire on the second day (aged 60). He was the first higher ranking soldier to be killed in the battle of Verdun.

Here you will find his memorial (the final site of his remains). Standing across the road looking at the memorial, behind you is a track taking you to two of his three grave sites (he

was disinterred twice). However, perhaps more interesting is his command post which is behind the memorial walking at a 2 o'clock angle behind the memorial. All around are the bunkers and shell holes of the battle. Allow 1 hour

----

<u>Douaumont Destroyed Village (DV) (27)</u> (Coordinates 49°13'10"N, 005°25'54"E – 49.21944, 5.43166) To the left of Ossuary.

www.alamy.com - E2FR7G

Another Destroyed Village with the staple chapel. Again the grounds are littered with shell craters. Worth a quick look.

<u>The Trench of Bayonettes (MEM) (28)</u> is just around the corner from the ossuary – a small concrete structure. Although it is famous –

said, erroneously, to be where a trench line of French soldiers were buried alive, leaving just their bayonets visible - it is poorly signed and explained and just contains a number of crosses (I gather the bayonets were gradually stolen as trophies by souvenir hunters). It is currently being refurbished and it is very underwhelming. It was paid for, long ago, by a wealthy American who believed this myth, and for a reason unknown to me still appears in guidebooks.

Fort Vaux (FAO) (29)
Address: 55400 Vaux-devant-Damloup
Coordinates: 49°12'00"N, 005°28'13"E – 49.20000, 5.47027

Slightly smaller than Fort Douaumont, though still enormous, this nearby fort held out for longer as it was properly garrisoned and supplied. However, it was besieged, and the battle was eventually waged inside the fort.

The commander of the fort, Major Raynal, fought alongside his men in a desperate struggle, latterly without food or water. It's worth remembering that food and especially water were in very short supply and many capitulations happened due to hunger and

thirst. Raynal's communication with his superiors was by the use of homing pigeons, including the famous "Valiant" (pictured above). His last communication, attached to Valiant, ended with the immortal words "this is my last pigeon"! After the note was read by French HQ Valiant died – from gas poisoning. He (and I don't know what sex it was, so forgive the presumption) was awarded the France's highest award, The Legion of Honour, and stuffed – residing now in the Paris Postal Museum. The underground galleries are preserved and open to the public. There is an entrance charge (reduced if seeing this and Fort Douaumont together). Allow 1 hour.

Ouvrage Bezonvaux (FAO) (30)
Address: Bezonvaux
Coordinates: 49°13'39"N, 005°28'07"E – 49.227500, 5.468611

This ouvrage is a severely damaged fort which is only partially visible. Most of it has been blown to dust, though what remains is almost an archeological dig. So get your wellies on, grab your torch and head on down. Don't expect lots of signboards – what you see is what you get. Bezonvaux is a ruined fort with trench systems leading to it and holes in the ground tempting balancing acts with cameras. Allow half an hour.

Bezonvaux Destroyed Village (DV) (31)
Address: Bezonvaux
Coordinates: 49°14'12"N, 005°28'05"E – 49.23666, 4.468055

 This is a particularly pretty Destroyed Village, with a stream running through it and the places where the house were originally sited are marked. Also here is a flavour of the people who lived here, with mementoes and photos. Well worth a stopover.

Mardi Gras Batterie (TTC) (32)
Address: Towards Etain on Left
Coordinates: 49°10'44"N, 005°28'43"E – 49.178888, 5.478611

These coordinates will get you to the exact spot up a track which is passable for cars, and my VW Golf did it, but only just! There is a tiny sign (are signs taxed

by the French on size?) and the battery is on the right hand side going upwards. Here are trenches leading to the battery, with shelters and gun emplacements. There are also holes in the ground leading to somewhere, but not accessible, though I could squeeze my camera in for a photo of a cavern. It certainly looks as if some have tried to enter, but it definitely doesn't look safe so please just look. There is much wreckage and iron fragments. Well worth stopping for a browse. Allow half an hour.

Fort Souville (FAO) (33)

Address: Near Douaumont

Coordinates: 49°11'10"N, 005°26'23"E – 49.186111, 5.439722

Please don't go here alone, and please don't forget your torch. This is the most dangerous of the forts I'll tell you about so I expect you'll do your own risk assessment. This fort is completely untouched, though it is signposted. The coordinates will get you

alongside it. The entrance is on the right and in front. On stepping into the darkness you are confronted immediately by a hole in the floor (see photo) which would put you a floor down. Inside it is very dark with rooms and corridors leading everywhere. Nothing is very safe here – and there is no lighting at all - so use your torches carefully to see

where you are going and what you are stepping into. Also check what the roof systems seem like – some are damaged and have collapsed. Some areas are concreted over to stop entry, but the floor is also dangerous as there is fallen masonry everywhere. There were quite a few other people when we went and it was useful to see others torches and recommendations as we explored. Afterwards you'll need a drink and you'll deserve one!

The Southern Sector

Voie Sacree (34)

[handwritten: D603 D1916]

The Sacred Way (or Road), the only real entry and exit for the French forces fighting in Verdun starts at the NVS to the south and becomes the D603 as it enters Verdun. Watch out for the cairns at the side of the road, as well as numerous memorials. It is the national road most well known in France – a road with another mythic stance.

[handwritten: Le Moulin Brule]

Ouvrage de la Falouse (FAO) (35)
Address: 55100
Coordinates: 49°07'27"N, 005°23'50"E – 49.12416, 5.39722
This site, just south of the town, between

Belleray south of the town, between Belleray and Dugny off the D301 (on a small track with

a small sign), is owned and run by the Verdun Rugby Club. So bear this in mind if you've got any complaints! This smaller ouvrage is, again, "still in the development stage". It's remarkable how something like this can still have so much original material in it. The mechanism for the

gun remains and there are rustic information cards to explain. Like any decent rugby club there is also a model French soldier getting off a toilet, and photo of French soldiers bathing in the river nude! This is a pay site, not expensive, but as it's pretty good, and as its run by Verdun Rugby, I'd say pay up 'cos the money's going to be used to further extend the site, and it's non- commercial. Given the number of forts and ouvrages which are explored in their untouched state, sometimes with ladders and ropes, this is one that is very original and untouched, whilst being totally legal! Allow about 1 hour. Small entrance charge.

In order to see the rest of the southern sector (often called the St Mihiel sector) – and it's yet more mind-blowing battlefields – head south from Verdun to St.Mihiel, about 20 miles. Be careful as directions will only appear once you are at the site. Therefore I have described exactly how to get to each of the next three sites. They are absolutely amazing, so do try to make the effort and time to get there. You won't be disappointed.

From St Mihiel take the D907 towards Apremont La Foret. After about two miles turn right on the D171c and follow this for about a mile to the Bois d'Ailly. On the left, where the forest begins, is a monument to the French 8th Corps. Stop here. Behind this is the Tranchee de la Soif.

Tranchee de la Soif (Trench of Thirst) (TTC) (36)

Address:Bois d'Ailly

Coordinates: 48°51'43"N, 005°33'58"E – 48.86194, 5.56611

The Bois d'Ailly is a trench system southwest

of St Mihiel, the scene of some of the most terrible fighting in the Great War. In mid-May a company of French Infantry under Commandant d'André reached the German fifth line but reinforcements couldn't be supplied, so they fell back, eventually holding a small section of trench. Without food or water they clung on, but eventually had to surrender. This is called the Trench of Thirst. The area of forest you walk through had some of the highest casualty rates, 60,000 French in this and the nearby woods alone. The trenches here are perhaps the best preserved original trenches on the whole of the Western Front. Allow 1 hour.

Once finished here return to the main road, the D907, and turn right, continuing for about a mile and a half to a right turn which is opposite a French unit memorial, to the Tranchee des Bavarois. Yet again, don't do this trench system alone!

Bavarian Trenches (TTC) (37)
Address: Bois d'Ailly
Coordinates: 48°51'36"N, 005°36'52"E – 48.86000, 5.61444

Threading through the forest these German trenches are very extensive and very deep. Some of the signage is helpful but there is much that you have to find yourselves. Some

trench sections are built of concrete blocks, well preserved. Be careful here as there are tunnels, some unprotected by grills, as well as very spikey barbed wire. A few sign boards tell the story of the trenches, but as you go deeper into the forest, following the trench line, just remember how to get back – rather bewildering. Allow 1 hour.

Return to the D907 and cross it, passing the memorial stone on the left, and head into the Foret de Gobessart. You only need to go about 800 yards, past the first crossing and a tiny sign for the German hospital is on your right. I spent much time travelling this side road trying to find this site. In the end I saw it was signposted with the smallest, most insignificant sign possible. But, believe me, this is a place worth finding.

Hospital Allemand (TTC) (38)
Address: Foret de Gobessart
Coordinates: 48°52'10"N, 005°37'04"E – 48.86944, 5.61777

 The hospital, a concrete block, consists of three rooms, with another sign warning not to enter! Once inside – you will be just as inquisitive as I was - it is damp and unsanitary. Walk on the top of the hospital and then you see what is not

immediately evident. It almost seems as if the hospital was built in and amongst a huge trench system. The trenches spread out from the hospital, but do be careful as there are unprotected tunnels here. But what a system! Allow 1 hour

----

Butte de Montsec (MEM) (39)
Address: 55300 Montsec
Coordinates: 48°53′22″N, 005°42′46″E – 48.8894, 5.7128
A stunning American memorial for all the US

troops who fought in the area, during the last period of the Great War. It's not just that it's a magnificent building, it's also in a position high on a hill, overlooking lakes and rivers. Circular, reminiscent of the Berkshire Memorial in Flanders "Plugstreet", but in a much improved situation, it has a real presence. The centre of the colonnade has a bronze relief map of the St Mihiel salient showing the military campaigns which took place in this area. It is a structure of great beauty and grandeur, totally dominating the countryside, and I usually plan to have a packed lunch sitting on the hill looking at the fantastic views all around.

St Mihiel U.S.A. Cemetery (MEM) (40)
Address: 54470 Thiaucourt
Coordinates: 48°57′22″N, 005°51′12″E – 48.95611, 5.85333

Beautiful white stone, lawns laid out to perfection. Another American Cemetery which allows you to stop, pause and reflect. This contains the graves of 4153 American military dead as well as a chapel and map building. The chapel contains beautiful mosaics.

Head back from here towards Verdun and see Les Eparges – another stunning battlefield.

Enter the village of Les Eparges and follow the D203 watching out for signs to Crete des Eparges. You will see the statue of the ghostly woman, head tilted back, eyes closed. Park at the base.

Les Eparges (TTC) (41)   *South*
Address: Les Eparges
Coordinates: 49°03′49″N, 005°36′35″E – 49.06361, 5.60972

This, a large memorial statue of a ghostly woman on a small hill, is the starting point for an amazing series of mine craters. At the bottom of the hill there are no pointers to the real action which is behind the statue. The first time I went nobody told me what to look for, so I returned from visiting a rather surreal sculpture. But the rather grotesque statue is just the start point. Continue for about half a kilometre directly away from the statue and the mine craters just get bigger and bigger. At the very end is a small car park and viewing point, with overgrown trenches. A terrible battle was fought here – do make  sure you have a look at photos of the area during the Great War, perhaps on google, being some of the most ghastly I've seen. This was a quagmire of mud, slime and death.

The size of the craters! The height of the trees in them! The steepness of the sides! It's a great walk. Allow 1 hour.

Forts and Ouvrages

The forts and ouvrages around Verdun are scattered like decaying confetti. There are so many of them (forty plus) that, apart from the most famous, they are rarely even signposted or highlighted. Yet these buildings, usually the size of Harrods, remain as reminders of the fear the French had of a German invasion from the east across their border. The most famous, Douaumont and Vaux, are easily accessible. However, all of them still remain as terrible relics, often deep in woods, covered in undergrowth, and nearly all are visible and explorable if you know where to find them.

To give an example, we were told of the Ouvrage of Le Poste de la Belle Epine. Following our SatNav we reached a path with a very small sign, and this came out at a concrete emplacement. The path, though overgrown, continued and so did we. At last the path fizzled out, with little to see through the moss and rotting foliage. As we were about to give up we became aware that the hill in front of us wasn't a hill but the ouvrage – covered in the same moss and dark green foliage. We were standing next to a fort, 130 years old, the size of a large office block, but now blending into the forest. This is typical of the forts and ouvrages. They are gigantic relics, built around the turn of the 20th century, built with reinforced concrete, which will continue to stand for generations.

I have listed them all here, along with their coordinates, so if you're an adventurous cove then go and have a peak. They aren't safe to enter, but they are fascinating to view. Do be very vigilant as they are usually very dodgy structures, but in their own unique way they are like coming across a pyramid for the first time – quite staggering, quite dark, quite stupendous and quite dangerous.

I have listed them all, roughly according to their geographic area. The map of the forts and ouvrages will also help to position them, but, to repeat, don't do these alone.

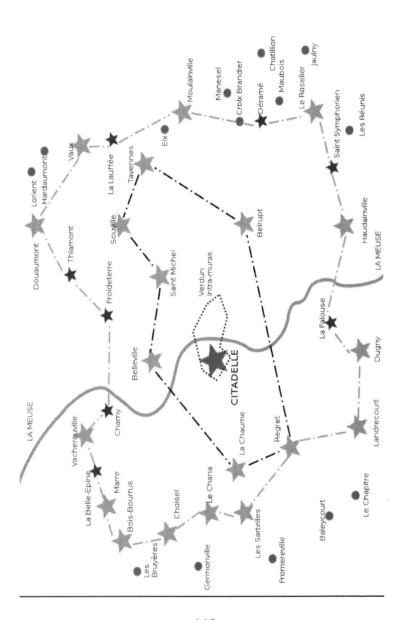

NORTH-EAST & NORTH-WEST Sector

Ouvrage de **Lorient**
>49°13′00″N, 005°27′40″E
>49.21666, 5.461111

Ouvrage du **Muguet**
>49°13′01″N, 005°27′54″E
>49.216944, 5.465000

Ouvrage de **Josemont**
>49°13′13″N, 005°27′50″E
>49.220277, 5.463888

Ouvrage de **Bezonvaux**
>49°13′42″N, 005°28′08″E
>49.228333, 5.468888

Ouvrage d'**Hardaumont**
>49°12′58″N, 005°28′12″E
>49.216111, 5.47000

Ouvrage de **Froideterre**
>49°11′51″N,005°24′13″E
>49.197500, 5.403611

Ouvrage de **Thiaumont**
>49°12′24″N, 005°25′09″E
>49.206666, 5.419166

Fort de **Douaumont**
>49°13′00″N, 005°26′20″E
>49.216666, 5.43888

Fort de **Vaux**
>49°12′01″N, 005°28′12″E
>49.200277, 5.47000

Ouvrage de La **Laufee**
>49°11′21″N, 005°28′53″E
>49.189166, 5.481388

Fort de **Belleville**
>49°10′50″N, 005°23′02″E
>49.180555, 5.383888

Fort **Saint-Michel**
>49°10′31″N, 005°24′52″E
>49.175277, 5.414444

Fort de **Souville**
>49°11′17″N, 005°26′23″E
>49.188055, 5.439722

Fort de **Tavannes**
>49°10′53″N, 005°27′47″E
>49.181388, 5.463055

Fort de **Moulanville**
>49°10′01″N, 005°29′12″E
>49.166944, 5.486666

SOUTH-EAST Sector

Ouvrage d'**Eix**
> 49°10'21"N, 005°28'56"E
> 49.172500, 5.482222

Ouvrage de **Croix-Brandier**
> 49°09'12"N, 005°28'56"E
> 49.153333, 5.482222

Ouvrage du **Manesel**
> 49°09'14"N, 005°29'58"E
> 49.153333, 5.499444

Ouvrage de **Chatillon**
> 49°08'28"N, 005°30'35"E
> 49.141111, 5.509722

Ouvrage de **Maubois**
> 49°08'16"N, 005°29'29"E
> 49.137777, 5.491388

Ouvrage de **Jaulny**
> 49°07'38"N, 005°30'37"E
> 49.127222, 5.510277

Ouvrage des **Bois-Reunis**
> 49°06'58"N, 005°28'19"E
> 49.116111, 5.471944

Ouvrage de **Derame**
49°08'38"N, 005°28'54"E
49.143888, 5.481666

Fort du **Rozelier**
49°07'30"N, 005°28'49"E
49.125000, 5.480277

Ouvrage de **Saint-Symphorien**
49°07'05"N, 005°27'20"E
49.118055, 5.455555

Fort de **Houdainville**
49°06'55"N, 005°26'00"E
49.115277, 5.433333

Fort de **Belrupt**
49°08'54"N, 005°26'02"E
49.148333, 5.433888

SOUTH-WEST Sector

Ouvrage du **Bois-du-Chapitre**
49°06'55"N, 005°18'48"E
49.115277, 5.313333

Ouvrage de **Baleycourt**
49°07'29"N, 005°18'08"E
49.124722, 5.302222

Ouvrage du **Bois-des-Sartelles**

49°08'50"N, 005°17'18"E

49.147222, 5.288333

Ouvrage de **Germonville**

49°10'09"N, 005°17'15"E

49.169166, 5.287500

Ouvrage des **Bruyeres**

49°11'14"N, 005°17'02"E

49.187222, 5.283888

Ouvrage de La **Falouse**

49°07'14"N, 005°24'02"E

49.120555, 5.400555

Fort de **Dugny**

49°06'45"N, 005°22'44"E

49.112500, 5.378888

Fort De **Landrecourt**

49°06'44"N, 005°20'35"E

49.112222, 5.343055

Fort de **Regret**

49°08'06"N, 005°20'15"E

49.135000, 5.337499

Poste puis fort des **Sartelles**

49°09'11"N, 005°18'35"E

49.153055, 5.309722

Fort de la **Chaume**

> 49°09'23"N, 005°19'46"E
>
> 49.156388, 5.329444

Poste puis fort du **Chana**

> 49°09'52"N, 005°18'36"E
>
> 49.164444, 5.31000

Poste puis fort du **Choisel**

> 49°10'42"N, 005°18'11"E
>
> 49.178333, 5.303055

Fort de **Bois-Bourrus**

> 49°11'30"N, 005°17'57"E
>
> 49.191666, 5.299166

Fort de **Marre**

> 49°11'44"N, 005°18'52"E
>
> 49.195555, 5.314444

Poste de **Belle-Epine**

> 49°11'59"N, 005°19'51"E
>
> 49.199722, 5.330833

Fort de **Vacherauville**

> 49°12'15"N, 005°20'31"E
>
> 49.204166, 5.341944

Ouvrage de **Charny**

> 49°12'01"N, 005°21'13"E
>
> 49.200277, 5.353611

Epilogue

Well – for this third edition that is enough. Enjoy your trip and I know you'll return.

Once visited, Verdun gets under your skin and you can't stop scratching. I expect to add and subtract as the years pass as I suspect there are magnificent finds still to come, especially with more trenches and tunnels being excavated. Whereas Flanders and The Somme have been pretty closely examined and prodded, the region around Verdun has many more secrets still to be surrendered.

I look forward to meeting people in one of the

Verdun pubs, where we can share our stories and experiences. The pubs of Verdun are the 21st Century equivalent of the 18th Century coffee houses of London. But just don't expect to meet Samuel Johnson there.

Verdun is so different, so raw, so unsanitised - it is the Great War battlefield without the tidying tinsel of our health and safety obsessed age.

You'll never forget Verdun.

For further Information and free maps
Maison de Tourisme Verdun
Place de la Natio, BP 232
55100 VERDUN TEL: 0033 3.29.86.14.18

Further Reading

Horne, Alistair, The Price of Glory: Verdun 1916, 1993 (for a detailed and yet very readable history of Verdun in the Great War)

Holstein, Christina, Walking Verdun, A Guide to the Battlefield, 2009

Jankowski, Paul, Verdun: The longest battle of the Great War, 2014

Holstein, Christina, Fort Douaumont, 2010

Coombs, Rose E B, Before Endeavours Fade, 1990

Also by
Stuart Townsend
Asylum Bound

Index

Index

Index

Index

Index

Index

Acknowledgements

My thanks go to my sister, Ruth for her ideas, proof reading and editing, to Simon for his cover design work, to Roger for being the original navigator and my co-explorer, to Bill for his specialist editing and to my long suffering wife Karen for allowing me leave of absence to explore the battlefields in France.

Special thanks to Mark for his phenomenal

expertise in all things computers and coordinates, along with his ability to translate my spidery, hand drawn, map to reality in this book.

Lastly special thanks to all those in Verdun who have helped with this project – from the staff in the museums to the French enthusiasts who advise me on the sites, to the Verdun Tourist Office and to Jean-Paul at the Romagne 14-18 Museum.

18499935R00076

Printed in Great Britain
by Amazon